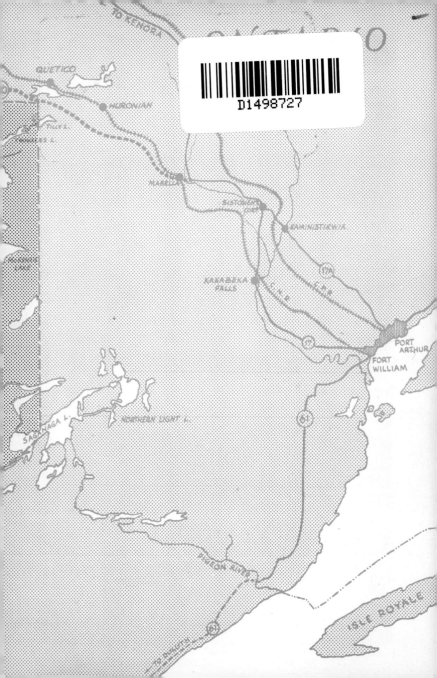

The Indians of Quetico

OJIBWA CAMP, EARLY NINETEENTH CENTURY

Artist unknown. From the Sigmund Samuel Canadiana Gallery of the
Royal Ontario Museum

THE INDIANS OF
QUETICO

BY EMERSON S. COATSWORTH

From field notes and research by
ROBERT C. DAILEY

4278

PUBLISHED FOR THE QUETICO FOUNDATION
BY UNIVERSITY OF TORONTO PRESS
1957

Quetico Foundation Series

Number One

The generous financial support of
Household Finance Corporation of
Canada, which made publication of
this book possible, is gratefully
acknowledged

Foreword

THIS is the first of a series of monographs sponsored by The Quetico Foundation. We feel it will be of general interest but is primarily designed to add to the pleasure of those who travel through the Quetico. Because neither the Quetico nor The Quetico Foundation is well known, it seems appropriate to give a word of explanation.

Some years ago a group of Canadian canoe men, admittedly mostly of the armchair variety, formed a committee to co-operate with the Ontario Department of Lands and Forests and with a United States committee appointed by President Roosevelt to preserve and promote the appreciation of the scenic, recreational, and historical value of the Quetico–Superior area. The Right Honourable Vincent Massey, C.H., was the first Chairman. After he became Governor General of Canada and consequently resigned from this office, The Quetico Foundation was chartered with similar objects and he graciously consented to be its patron.

The Quetico or Quetico–Superior area extends from Rainy Lake to Lake Superior, and includes that vast wilderness in Minnesota and Ontario through which the International Boundary follows the highway of the early fur traders. This ran from Grand Portage, near the spot where the Pigeon River empties into Lake

Superior, westward to Fort Frances and International Falls.

Almost fifty years ago, by a little known but remarkably wise piece of international co-operation, there was set aside, on the Canadian side, what is now the Quetico Provincial Park and at the same time, contiguously on the United States side, the Superior National Forest. Because the Precambrian Shield, which has given Canada so much of its mineral wealth and so much of its magnificent canoe country, only makes one shallow dip south of the border, the scenic beauty that it has brought to the Superior National Forest, because of its rarity, is far better known in the United States than is the Quetico Provincial Park in Canada. A primary purpose of the Quetico Foundation is to help Canadians realize what a valuable asset they have, that its primitive beauty has remained almost unspoilt, thanks to the vision of the Ontario Lands and Forests Department, and that this unique Park is now readily accessible from Canada.

Those who get the most pleasure out of travel equip themselves with some knowledge of the people who in the past have travelled over the same trails. Before, during, and after the days of the early explorers and the fur traders, there were the Indians. A few still live in the Quetico, though not in the Park, but their forebears have left evidence of their habits and mode of living. Some of this evidence cannot be fully explained, but all of it is interesting.

The field notes and research, together with the line drawings, were contributed by Robert C. Dailey, who, with his wife, spent a summer in the area preparing material for a lengthier treatment of the subject. Mr. Dailey is a graduate student at the University of Toronto, specializing in Anthropology. Mr. E. S. Coatsworth has a special interest in the subject of the North American Indian and, thanks to his writing skill and scholarship and the contributions of Mr. Dailey, the result is authoritative and entertaining and will add immeasurably to the enjoyment of all those in whom the Indian way of life arouses curiosity, and particularly those who read it in relation to a canoe trip in the Quetico.

Other monographs on the features of this fascinating international wilderness are already in preparation.

For the Quetico Foundation

HAROLD C. WALKER
Chairman

Contents

FOREWORD   v

PLATES   x

Introduction   3

Social Organization   5

Family Life   8

The Cycle of Life   14

The Quest for Food   19

From Raw Materials to Finished Products   27

The World of the Supernatural   43

Epilogue   54

QUETICO PARK   57

ACKNOWLEDGEMENTS   58

Plates

FRONTISPIECE

Ojibwa Camp, Early Nineteenth Century

BETWEEN PAGES 6 AND 7

Wild Rice
Peaked Lodge

BETWEEN PAGES 22 AND 23

River Rapids
Picture Rock
Pictograph
Ojibwa Grave

BETWEEN PAGES 38 AND 39

Chatterton Falls
The End of a Portage

The Indians of Quetico

Introduction

WHEN the first white explorers reached the Quetico Park region west of Lake Superior in the seventeenth century, the Indians they met called themselves "Outchibouac." Since these Indians did not possess a written language, their tribal name has come to be spelled in several ways. In the United States the most commonly used variant is "Chippewa," and in Canada "Ojibwa." The Canadian variant will be used throughout this book.

The Ojibwa were the most recent Indians to arrive in the Quetico country. The first to come, in the considered opinion of archaeologists, arrived at least five thousand years ago, and in the centuries which have passed, other groups have come and gone. Most, if not all, were nomadic hunters and collectors, depending on the wild game and the wild plants which provided their food. A few had mastered the rudiments of agriculture.

Today, there are no longer any Ojibwa Indians living permanently within the borders of Quetico Park. Ownership of the land, in Canada at least, passed by treaty to the white man in 1873, and the Ojibwa who remain in the region are to be found on reserves north, east, and west of the Park.

What sort of people were these Ojibwa of the seventeenth century, the people whose life will be described in this book? Their way of life has all but vanished, and it differed radically from our own. They succeeded in adapting themselves exceedingly well to their environment, developing many skills which are, unfortunately, rapidly being forgotten. They were essentially a nomadic people, living for the most part in small family groups. In coming to terms with their environment they lived in close harmony with nature and with spiritual forces. It is difficult for modern industrial man to appreciate just how close, how intimate this relationship was. The Ojibwa were, indeed, a part of their environment, and felt as one with the rocks and water, the trees and plants, the birds and animals which they could see around them, and with the unseen forces of the supernatural which affected their lives at every turn.

There is much that was of value in the life of the Ojibwa, not the least of which was an outlook on life and a relationship with nature which we might do well to reflect on. We, as the bearers of western civilization, have by no means succeeded in solving the basic problems which beset mankind, and are, at this particular time in our history, in danger of bringing about our own destruction. It is worth our while, therefore, to pause and examine the life of a people who were able to live in such close harmony with the realities of nature—just as it is well worth our while to preserve the last stretches of wilderness country such as Quetico Park whence such a way of life developed.

Social Organization

THE SOCIAL WORLD of the Ojibwa may be considered from the aspect of the tribe, of the clan, or of the small local group. We must be careful in using the word "tribe," for, although there are today approximately forty thousand Indians in the region surrounding the Great Lakes who refer to themselves by the name "Ojibwa," they are not, and never have been, a cohesive political entity, despite the customs, beliefs, language, and way of life which they held in common. Rather, they comprised many local groups quite independent of one another—so much so that warfare between two geographically separated groups was not unknown. We shall therefore pass on from the tribal distinction, for we are considering, at most, the few hundred Ojibwa who lived in the particular region we know as Quetico Park.

The second aspect—that based upon membership in the clan—is one which is unknown among ourselves, but which is observed by many other peoples throughout the world. This form of social distinction must not be confused with the clan system of the Scottish Highlands, which really consists of a series of small tribes.

The symbol of the clan was the totem, and every Ojibwa belonged from birth to one of several clans, each of which possessed its own distinct totemic emblem. This emblem, or symbol, usually represented a familiar forest animal. The Ojibwa believed that in those days of long ago, just after the creation of the world we know today, the animals which they recognized as their clan symbols lived as their own ancestors. In other words, they believed they were descended from a number of common forest animals. Many myths grew up concerning these ancestral animals and how they had come into being. Many of the clan names used by the Ojibwa are those associated with the wildlife of Quetico Park today: bear, moose, eagle, loon, crane (heron), and catfish.

An important aspect of the clan organization was that marriage between two people belonging to the same clan was forbidden. Thus, when an Ojibwa youth wished to marry, he had to seek his partner from another clan. This prohibition can be understood when it is realized that members of a clan—because of the myths of the era of creation—thought of themselves as being related. There was no biological basis for this belief of course, but the bonds which linked clan members together were very strong—stronger, in many cases, than the ties which held together the biological family. It is said, for example, that if an Ojibwa were to witness a quarrel developing between a man who belonged to his clan, and one of his own blood relatives who belonged to another clan, social convention would dictate that the bystander side in with his clansman against his blood relative, despite the fact that the bystander might conceivably never have seen his clansman before.

Clan membership was inherited and passed down from one generation to the next through the father.

WILD RICE

A wild rice marsh in Quetico Park. So important was the harvesting
of this staple crop to the Ojibwa that they referred to September as
"The Moon When the Wild Rice Is Harvested"

PEAKED LODGE

A present-day Ojibwa peaked lodge used by a hunter in winter. The lodge poles are partially covered with spruce boughs for better protection against snow and wind

Children, therefore, always belonged to the clans of their fathers and never to those of their mothers.

The third aspect of Ojibwa social organization was the small local group. For the greater part of the year this group consisted of the family: the husband, the wife, their children, and perhaps the husband's parents. The family was a very closely knit social unit and, except in spring and perhaps early summer, lived in its own encampment—often in a single dwelling—isolated by the intervening forest from the nearest neighbouring family group.

Because of this isolation, the livelihood of the family depended to a very considerable extent upon the resourcefulness of its members, and for this reason the family was the most important social unit in Ojibwa life. In the spring, however, several family groups—varying from perhaps three to fifteen—would come together in the maple forests to collect maple sap. The size of the encampment would, for a few weeks, increase in size, and a form of village life would appear. Leadership would rest with the head of one of the families gathered together. But as summer advanced the larger encampments would break up into the smaller family groups again, when the people dispersed to continue the annual cycle of life.

In brief, then, the human world for the average Ojibwa was limited by the size of the family to which he belonged for most of the year. For a few weeks in spring and early summer, his social world would increase several times—but only to shrink back again for the remainder of the year to the limits of the single family.

Family Life

THE OJIBWA FAMILY, as we have just seen, was the small social group which was the primary fact of wilderness life. It was continually on the move in search of the foods on which it subsisted, but despite this movement it was stable and followed well-established patterns. However, before discussing family life let us look at the dwellings which housed the families in the Ojibwa encampments.

There were several types of dwellings, but the two most commonly built and lived in were the dome-

shaped wigwam and the peaked lodge. The dome-shaped wigwam could be built easily and quickly. A framework of slender poles would be erected around a ground area measuring approximately ten feet by twelve on the average. The trunk ends of the poles would be driven firmly into the ground, and the upper ends drawn down and inward toward one another, and tied to form the frame for the dome or arch of the wigwam. Two rows of cross poles would then be lashed to these uprights, the first about three feet from the ground and the second about six. At one end an opening would be left below the lower cross pole level to allow for a doorway. The sides of the wigwam would then be covered with mats woven from bulrushes, which would be hung in overlapping fashion over the cross poles. The roof frame would then be covered with sheets of birchbark which had previously been stitched together. At the peak of the dome a hole would be left between intersecting rolls of bark to allow the smoke to escape. The doorway would be covered with a separate woven rush mat, or by a cover of sewn deer or moose hides.

The peaked lodge was similar in shape to our modern wedge tent. The framework would be made of a series of crossed poles, each driven firmly into the ground at one end and lashed together near the tops where they intersected, so that they would support a ridge pole. This framework would then be covered with rolls of birchbark, with entrance ways at one or at either end. Since there would be cracks at the peak between the sheets of bark where the cross poles met the ridge pole, it was not necessary to provide a special smoke hole.

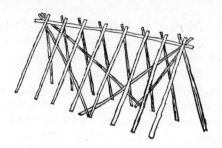

Peaked lodges varied considerably in length. They were usually built to accommodate one family, but early white travellers have reported seeing peaked lodges containing up to four fireplaces, indicating the presence of at least four families.

The interior of an Ojibwa dwelling was laid out according to a plan, a traditional plan which gave each age group of the family its area in which to sit. The children's place was near the centre, closest to the fire. The mother and father would sit on either side of the doorway, and the grandparents across from them at the rear. This plan enabled the grown-ups to keep watchful eyes on the younger folk, who were thus forced to pass their parents in entering or leaving the home.

The fireplace in the centre of the dwelling was kept smouldering all day and night, and was attended to by the women. The womenfolk prepared the meals and were responsible for many other tasks, including the making of clothing, curing meat, setting out traps for fish and small game, embroidering, tanning leather, preparing twine, brewing native dyes, cleaning and mending the men's hunting equipment, making their own cooking utensils, weaving nets and mats, gathering

10

birchbark, erecting the dwellings, tilling the gardens (if any), collecting wild food plants—and caring for their children. Women were assisted by their daughters in these multitudinous tasks, while young boys helped their fathers. By comparison, the father's duties were fewer in number, but they were more active in nature, for he was the hunter and trapper. This division of labour threw equal responsibility on both sexes for the well-being of the family groups.

Ojibwa dwellings were often crowded to the point where it was impossible to make room indoors for storage purposes. Therefore the Indians built racks or shelves on frame tripods outside in the open, so that foodstuffs could be kept until needed. The racks were built high enough off the ground to keep the food safe from dogs and rodents.

Indoors, cedar boughs were spread and covered over with rush mats to give protection from the bare ground. At night the Indians covered themselves with blankets sewn from the hides of animals. These skins would be tanned but would still retain the hair. In daytime these blankets would be rolled up and placed along the walls for seats.

A winter's night in Quetico can be intensely cold, but Ojibwa lodges were nonetheless kept reasonably warm and comfortable. Many of the fondest memories an Indian possessed were probably of winter evenings spent around the wigwam fire listening to the stories of wonder related by grandparents—stories of Indian life, the forest, and the spirits who dwelt there. When the stories came to an end the Indians would remove their moccasins, loosen their outer clothing, and lie down to sleep in their blankets, with their feet toward the fire. If the weather were unusually bitter or stormy, one of the grandparents might remain awake to watch the fire, feeding it when it burned low to maintain the warmth. In summer, however, the Ojibwa invariably slept out of doors.

Like other peoples, the Ojibwa found time for recreation. They were fond of games, both games of chance and those which called for physical dexterity. Of the first type two were especially popular. One was the "moccasin game," a guessing game. An object would be hidden in one of a number of moccasins and the players would have to decide which moccasin did, or which moccasins did not, contain the hidden article. The other game was played with a bowl and seven circular bone counters which were painted black on one side and various bright colours on the other sides. The bowl would be struck on the ground (which was usually covered by a blanket) by a player so that the counters inside it would bounce up into the air and fall back down into the bowl. Scoring was done on the basis of the colour combinations of the counters agreed on before the play.

Games calling for physical dexterity were numerous, and one of the most popular was lacrosse, which has of course been adopted long since by the white man. The

12

Ojibwa original of this game, however, was much rougher than our modern version, and physical injury during play occurred frequently.

Dancing, which to the Ojibwa had considerable ceremonial significance, was also a popular form of recreation. Story-telling, as we have already mentioned, was a form of recreation too. It was practised all year round, but was particularly popular during cold winter evenings when the Indians were confined to their wigwams after the long and arduous day. The stories they told were for amusement, but they also served to pass along from one generation to the next the oral traditions of the tribe. As such, story-telling played an important part in Ojibwa life. The tales which were repeated were many and varied, some evoking the golden age when the world was young and others illustrating the prowess of contemporary hunters. But all stories emphasized and reflected the Ojibwa feeling of nearness and relatedness to the animals, the forest, and the supernatural.

The Cycle of Life

THE CYCLE OF LIFE, for a newly born Ojibwa baby, began in a cradle board, a piece of wood about two feet long, one foot wide, and an inch thick. He would spend his first year on this board, comfortably wrapped and prevented from slipping off by a curved piece of wood at the bottom which confined his feet, and by bands which were attached to the sides. His parents would want him to grow up straight in stature and restrained in action, and the cradle board served to start this training.

We have mentioned the importance of the supernatural in Ojibwa life, and the attitude of "oneness" which the adult Indian maintained with regard to himself, his fellow Ojibwa, his natural environment, and the supernatural. Religion and magic were vital to him in establishing contact with the supernatural, and these were introduced to him while he was still on the cradle board and, of course, long before he was conscious of them. His parents, believing that spirits which held power over human life were ever present, sought to attract benevolent powers to ensure his health and proper guidance—and also sought, at the same time, to dispel those spirits they believed to be evil. To achieve this they would make use of the wooden hoop which was fixed to the cradle board at right angles for purposes of lifting and carrying. This hoop would, of course, support extra coverings for the baby and trinkets to amuse him, but, more important, it would serve to hold two other types of attachments. The first would consist of charms—a small sack containing a piece of the baby's umbilical cord (to bring wisdom) and a small circle of wood several inches in diameter filled with strands of sinew to stimulate a spider's web (to catch evil spirits which might harm the baby). The second type of attachment would consist of gifts presented by the person whom the parents had chosen to name him.

A similar magical practice was followed to hurry the baby's growth. Soon after birth he would be fitted with a pair of tiny moccasins in which a number of holes had purposely been cut in the soles. These holes were to indicate to the spirits that the baby needed new moccasins, and to hurry him along to the walking stage so that he might have them.

Parents would bestow a name on their baby, but more important than this name, from the point of view of the child's relationship with the supernatural, would be his ceremonial name. This would be given by an individual chosen by the parents because of the spirit power which he had received in dreams. The Ojibwa attached great importance to dreams, believing that through them the guardian spirit—which every Ojibwa wished to possess—would manifest itself. Dreams with spiritual significance were those in which such natural phenomena as rain, lightning, thunder, waterfalls, and birds and animals appeared. The parents would consider very carefully the question of a suitable ceremonial name-giver, and would search out a man or woman whose own spirit power had been proven through the achievement of remarkable feats of hunting or in the curing of disease. When the most suitable name-giver had been found the ceremony would be conducted, and in this way the parents believed that some of the name-giver's own spirit power would be transferred to their baby, thereby ensuring a safe and successful life in the years to come.

Ojibwa parents were extremely fond of their children, and this feeling was reciprocated as the young ones grew up. Children were treated gently, tactfully, yet firmly, and were constantly reminded of those things which the parents considered essential to their well-being. Their deportment was a serious consideration, but in the course of training, physical cruelty was never applied. Fear might be used, especially with recalcitrant children, but never to the extent of producing a loss of self-confidence. One of the greatest forces in child training, especially in the field of ethics, was that of public opinion. There was no privacy within the family wigwam during the seasons of isolation in the forest, and very little during the few weeks when several families lived together in a small cluster of wigwams in a common encampment. Everyone knew what everyone else was doing or had done, and in most instances the threat of gossip alone was enough to deter questionable behaviour.

Children were allowed to play freely, but their training for adult life was begun, in a modest way, almost as soon as they were able to run about. Little girls gradually learned household duties from their mothers, and their brothers were taught the rudiments of hunting, trapping, snaring, stalking, and how to observe the habits and movements of animals. They also learned the techniques of magic which were necessary to attract wild game. Early training for both sexes was quite essential among the Ojibwa, for marriage took place at a relatively early age. Newly-weds would be expected to set up their own households within a year of marriage, and, since they would be isolated from all other family groups for many months of the year, their lives would depend upon the efficiency with which each partner performed his duties.

The behaviour of young people was strictly regulated until marriage. A suitor, before he could talk to the girl of his choice, would first have to receive the permission of her parents—even to enter their wigwam. But once he had indicated his intentions of marrying, he would be allowed greater latitude in conducting his courtship. He would signify his intention by killing a deer or other large animal and presenting it to the girl's parents, as proof of his ability as a hunter and his willingness to provide for his prospective wife. If his proposal were accepted, he would be invited to join the family in eating the meat of the animal he had killed. After marriage the young man would live with his wife in her parents' wigwam, and it would be his duty to supply them with their meat for about one year. When this period had elapsed he would be free to take his wife away and set up his own household.

At death, just as at birth, an Ojibwa was the object of a ceremony. The death rites were to ensure that the newly released spirit would safely enter the spirit world and begin a new, long, and successful life in that unknown and unseen land. It was just as important to ensure that his spirit would not take offence at any actions of those Indians whom he had left behind in this world and attempt to wreak vengeance upon them. A close friend of the dead man would deliver a eulogy, and the ceremony would be accompanied by drumming, the shaking of rattles, and wailing. The dead one would be mourned, but he would also be given courage and a reminder that he had now joined the great company of spirits which had preceded him into the next world, including many of his own friends and relatives.

The body of a dead man would be carefully washed and dressed in his finest clothes, and his hair braided. His face and clothing would often be painted with a brown pigment and his body left for a full day in the wigwam. Then, wrapped in animal skins and surrounded by objects which had been his favourites during life—and almost invariably including his pipe and tobacco pouch—the body would be placed either on a simple wooden platform and lodged in the fork of a tree, or buried in a shallow grave in the ground. After the coming of the white man, when sawn lumber became available, the Ojibwa would often build small shrine-like boxes over graves, where, they felt, the souls of the departed might dwell.

The Quest for Food

THE SEARCH FOR FOOD was the main occupation of the Ojibwa and whatever the season, they would devote a very considerable part of the working day to this task. They were primarily hunters and collectors of wild food products and, as such, they depended completely upon their natural environment for everything they ate.

There were two consequences of this dependence. The first was that they were obliged to move from place to place as the seasons changed in order to find their food. Secondly, their diet would vary considerably from season to season, and it was often necessary for them to live mainly upon one staple food at a time.

Their staples were meat, fish, wild rice, and maple sugar. Some groups did manage to cultivate the soil in spite of their general nomadic habits, and grew corn, beans, pumpkins, and squash. Sometimes tobacco was grown as well.

Let us examine the yearly food-gathering cycle by starting with spring, at the time when the snows of winter were beginning to melt. The family groups which had been hunting and trapping all winter independently of one another would now forgather in the maple groves to collect the sap which was rising in the sugar maples. Each family possessed the right to a portion of the "sugar bushes" in a particular region, a property right handed down in the male line over the generations.

The processes of collecting and boiling down sap into syrup and sugar were tedious. They left very little time for recreation, but they were nonetheless enjoyable, for they heralded the approach of warmer weather and added a welcome touch of sweetness to the diet. The sap was collected in bark vessels which, between seasons, were stored away in small shelters in the forest. The Ojibwa made a granulated sugar similar to our own and, as well, a sugar like our own hard candy, which they would set out to harden in the cool air in birchbark moulds. Maple sugar was a staple, as we have said, but it was also used to provide seasoning for fruits, vegetables, cereals, and even fish.

The close relationship we have noticed which bound man, nature, and the supernatural into a single, intimate world, could be seen in the quest for food. The Indians would offer to the spirits a portion of the maple sap they had collected, just as, later in the year, they would offer them the first fruits of every wild crop they harvested.

When the sap had been collected the little village encampments of several families would begin to disappear again. Those families which practised agriculture would go to the grounds which, like the maple groves, were theirs to cultivate. They broke the ground and hoed it with wooden implements and planted their crops in little hillocks, or in circular-shaped patches three or four feet in diameter.

During the summer months there were a number of wild crops for the Ojibwa to harvest. The blueberry crop was of great importance, and they also gathered chokecherries, June berries, wild raspberries, and low bush cranberries. Seasonings, too, would be harvested, including wild ginger, bearberry, and mountain mint. The Indians would also use these seasonings to make beverages. They would be added to water, boiled, and set aside to cool. Acorns and bulrushes (roots) were also gathered as food products.

In late September the Ojibwa harvested another of their staple crops, the wild rice. This crop was just as important or, if not more important than, the sap which they collected in the spring, and it marked the end of the annual growing cycle. This crop was a crucial one and, if by chance as sometimes happened it was destroyed by windstorms, some of the families would surely be visited by famine before spring. So important was this harvest that the Indians named September "The Moon When The Wild Rice Is Harvested." It was a time of festival, a social and religious occasion, when thanks were rendered to the spirits for their bounty, and was thus similar in many ways to our own thanksgiving celebrations.

Each family possessed hereditary rights to a section of the marshy land where the wild rice grew—marshes such as the one in Kawa Bay on Kawnipi Lake. The harvesting was done by the women, who would make their way through the wild rice plants in their canoes. Usually there would be two women to each canoe. The woman in the stern would move the craft with a long pole, for the plant growth would be too heavy to permit paddling, and the woman in the bow would reach out with one hand and bend the rice stalks over and into

the canoe, so that she could knock off the kernels with a stick which she would be holding in her other hand. Later, on shore, the kernels would be dried on sheets of birchbark, parched over fire to loosen the husks, and then pounded with a wooden pestle. The husks would be removed by winnowing and the rice stored away for the winter in birchbark containers. When eaten, the rice might be boiled in water, or used as the base of a

RIVER RAPIDS

A typical rapids on the Maligne River. Lakes and rivers were the
"water highways" of the Ojibwa, which they traversed in their
birchbark canoes

PICTURE ROCK

An example of the type of overhanging rocky cliff which the Ojibwa
would select for their pictographs, or rock paintings

PICTOGRAPH

A portrayal of the thunderbird, executed by an Ojibwa centuries
ago on the face of an overhanging rocky cliff. Such pictures seldom
exceeded twelve inches in height or width

OJIBWA GRAVE

An example of the structures Ojibwa began building over the graves of their dead—to accommodate departed spirits—once the sawn lumber of the white man's mills became available

broth, or simply eaten dry. It was also used to season wild fowl, a custom we have adopted from the Indians.

Corn, the chief cultivated crop, was prepared and eaten in a number of ways. It could be ground by pounding in a wooden mortar with a wooden pestle. It could be parched or roasted in the husk or boiled. Pumpkins and squash were either eaten when ripe or dried and stored for winter use. Wild plants which were harvested were also stored away for winter use in underground pits. These pits would be dug to a depth of about six feet and lined with sheets of birchbark. When the food had been placed inside, it would be covered over with more sheets of birchbark and, as a further protection against animals and weather, covered again with hay, a layer of wooden beams or logs, and finally a layer of earth. Thus stored, food would keep for many months. When taken out for eating these dried vegetables would be mixed with water and heated. The heating was usually done by placing hot stones in the wooden or bark bowls along with the water and vegetables.

Fish could be caught in all seasons. The lakes and rivers of Quetico were as well stocked in the seventeenth century as they are today, and in winter the fisherman would spear his catch through holes in the ice. He would often attract the fish with artificial lures

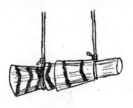

which he had carved of wood. Because of the season, he could store away his fish for weeks or even months. The Ojibwa, incidentally, also collected and enjoyed fish eggs.

Summer fishing would begin when the maple sap had been collected. Each family as it moved off to collect the fruits of the forest would camp by a likely fishing spot, for this type of food was a summer staple. Both men and women took part in this activity, and as the summer advanced they would intensify their efforts, so that some of the catch could be dried and stored away for the coming winter. They caught their fish, for the greater part, with nets and seines, but like ourselves they would also use lines and hooks, and would sometimes fish from their canoes. At night they would attract fish by the light of torches and catch them with spears.

When the autumn frosts gave warning of winter's approach the Ojibwa families would move on to their winter hunting camps, from which, after the arrival of the white traders, they would also conduct their winter trapping activities. Hunting was not confined to winter by any means, but the trapping of fur-bearing animals was done chiefly during this season.

The animals the Indians depended upon for food were varied. Perhaps their main quarry were the deer, moose, and bear which they killed with bow and arrows. The meat would be boiled or roasted if eaten soon after killing, but, if intended for storage, would be cut up into strips and dried over slow fires. They also snared rabbits and muskrat intensively and, to a lesser extent, otter and beaver. The fat in the tail of the beaver was considered a special delicacy. In winter, red, black, and silver-grey fox and timber, prairie, and brush wolves were sometimes hunted, and the hunter would pursue one of these animals over the deep snow on snowshoes until it lay exhausted from continually sinking in the snow, completely at the Indian's mercy. In spring and early summer wild ducks and pigeons were hunted, and caught either by snaring or shooting with bow and arrows.

The bow and arrow was the chief means of hunting, though for larger game the arrows were not designed to kill outright. They would cause the animal to bleed, and the hunter would pursue the wounded animal, perhaps for hours, until it fell from the loss of blood. The Ojibwa would also make artificial animal calls, just as we do today, and they would also use torches or jacklights to attract game at night—a practice which is now illegal.

The Ojibwa men, who were the trappers as well as the hunters, would catch large animals in "fall" traps. Such a trap would be activated by a trigger, which when released by an unsuspecting animal would cause a weighted log or timber to fall, pinning the animal to the ground and often breaking its back. Smaller animals, including otter, mink, beaver, and muskrat, were usually caught in nets made of nettle stalk fibre, while rabbits and winter birds were taken in snares.

The Ojibwa hunter was a skilled man, schooled from boyhood in the arts of observing, stalking, and killing. But to ensure success he would also use charms, which he would employ to help bring about the results he desired. These charms were designed to bring the myriad spirits—which controlled the natural world—to his assistance on the trail and thereby bring him good luck in his hunting. Most charms were made from herbs which had been dried and ground into fine powders. While in the forest the hunter would often stop and smoke some of these powders. In extreme cases, when families had little to eat and their survival depended entirely upon the luck of the hunters, the women and children would refrain from eating entirely and might paint their faces black—an indication of their penitence to the spirits they feared they had offended.

The Ojibwa, as a trapper, secured both food and fur from the animals he trapped, for the flesh of the fur-bearing animals was quite edible and always used for food. Trapping was almost always an individual occupation, and trap lines would extend for miles across the wilderness. Just as the family group in winter lived isolated from other families, so the trapper would spend many hours alone studying the movements and the habits of the game he sought. His family's dwelling would have been erected in some part of the Quetico where he expected game to be plentiful and he himself, since he was also the hunter of the family, would spend most of his time in the woods checking his traps and watching the trail for evidence of game.

From Raw Materials to Finished Products

FIRE, to the Ojibwa, was the gift of the spirits and the most useful tool he possessed. It enabled him to cook his food, warm his body, and light his pipe. Before the fur traders introduced flint and steel he would make fire, as a general rule, with what is known as the fire drill. He would produce friction by rotating a spindle or drill of ashwood on a hearthboard of cedar. He would place a ball of finely shredded bark so that it would ignite when the rotating movement had produced heat of the proper temperature.

The raw materials which the Ojibwa found of greatest use in making their tools and equipment were wood and stone. From the former they fashioned their bows and arrows, twine and thread, snowshoes, toboggans, sleds, drums, mats, containers, basketry—the list is virtually endless. From the latter they made their pipes and such tools as knives, axes, scrapers, and adzes. We shall consider a number of their manufactures to illustrate just how extensively the Ojibwa used these raw materials of wood and stone.

One of the most important articles used in daily life was twine. Its uses were many as we shall see. It was made, usually, from the fibrous inner bark of the basswood tree. To secure it an Indian would first have to remove the bark from the tree. He would do this by reaching up as high as he possibly could and making a cut with his knife straight down the trunk of the tree to the ground. He would then loosen the bark and, after removing it from the tree, would cut it lengthwise into strips each several inches wide. Then he would place these strips to soak in water, perhaps in a nearby pond, for at least two days. The soaking would soften the bark sufficiently to permit him to detach the outer bark leaving him with the soft and pliable inner layer of yellow fibre.

These strips of fibre would then be cut into very narrow shreds and dried. The fibre itself contains many layers which can easily be separated, and the extent of separation desired would depend upon the uses to which the fibre would be put. Basketry, for instance, called for the entire thickness of the fibre, while twine required merely one thin layer. For this latter purpose each strand would be separated at the middle and the split carried along to both ends. The thin layers which were produced in this way would be moistened and twisted to form a piece of cord the length of the original strip cut from the tree. If such a piece were not long enough for the purpose at hand, other pieces would be spliced on to produce the required length. When finished and dried twine of this type would withstand the strains of everyday use without pulling apart.

The fibre of the wood nettle was also used to make twine, although because of its finer texture it was more often used to make thread. To prepare it the stalk of the wood nettle fibre would be cut and split into the required diameters. It would then be treated in the same way as basswood fibre. Bowstrings were often made from this fibre too, and would be waxed or rubbed with pitch to make them waterproof.

Hunting bows were usually made of oak or ash. They varied in length, but on the average would measure about four feet. Sometimes they would be decorated with patterns etched with hot pointed stones and coloured with natural dyes. Bow strings might also be made from the neck skin of the snapping turtle, which would withstand great use and which would neither shrink nor stretch. The turtle's head would be cut off close to the shell and the skin removed. With a sharp knife the skin would be cut in circular or coil fashion to produce a long, continuous strip, which would then be twisted into a cord.

Arrows were fashioned from the stalks of the June berry bush and ground smooth in a grooved piece of sandstone. The flint arrowhead would be inserted in a notch cut in one end of the arrow and held in place by binding with sinew or strips of green bark. Arrows were of several types, depending upon their purpose. Those made to kill waterbirds were designed so that they would not sink if they missed their mark and fell into the water. Those intended for rabbits were tipped with turtle claws to increase their power of penetration, while those made to hunt deer were equipped with stone or bone heads fastened in such a way that the arrow shaft would pull out once the animal had been

hit and begun running through the woods. Because it would pull out, the shaft could not act as a plug, which might prevent the animal from bleeding to death. To guide the arrows through the air, eagle or hawk feathers would be bound to the shafts with sinew.

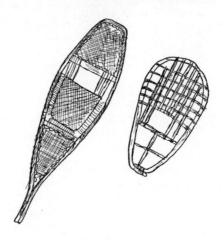

In winter the Ojibwa used snowshoes, toboggans, and sleds for transportation. Snowshoe frames were made of ash and laced with rawhide netting. Sometimes they were round in shape and sometimes oval, trailing off into tails. Some snowshoes were made with turned-up "toes." Toboggans were the most popular type of winter conveyance and were made of hardwood which had been cut during the winter months. The wood would be well soaked in hot water and heated in front of fires in order to curl up the front ends. Cleats would be placed along the sides and bottom so that the loads could be properly held in place. Sleds were made of ash: the runners would be steamed into U shapes to support the floor boards which were held in their places by cross-pieces. Both sleds and toboggans were pulled by teams of two or three dogs—the only animal which was domesticated by these people.

In summer the Ojibwa traversed the Quetico region by canoe, for the many lakes and rivers served them as "water highways." Their canoes were made from the bark of the birch tree and in shape were similar to our canoes of today—which, of course, are modelled after the Indian originals. The canoe, however, was not a pleasure craft to the Ojibwa: it was a necessity, and their only form of transportation when the waters were free of ice. The birch canoe was light and highly manoeuvrable, and an Indian would kneel on the floor to paddle, for it possessed neither centre-board nor seats.

Canoe bark was cut from the living tree in spring when the rising sap made it easy to peel the bark from the trunk. The ribs, thwarts, and gunwale framework were made of cedar and fashioned with great care to ensure that the finished craft would be properly balanced. The outline of the canoe was first staked out on the ground. The strips of bark were then set in place, supported by the stakes. Then an inner lining of flat pieces of wood was laid, and the pieces secured together and sewn to the ribs as well. The thwarts would be positioned and the canoe carefully inspected to make certain that every joint was properly sewn. Finally, every seam would be waterproofed with hot pine pitch.

As we have seen, the Ojibwa made great use of mats to cover the sides of their dwellings and to serve as

31

interior floor coverings. These mats were twined or woven from bulrushes or cedar bark. The strands would be woven while still moist and pliant on simple looms made of upright poles supported by top cross-pieces or, even more simply, from a single cross-piece lashed to two conveniently situated trees. The warp was made by attaching one row of strips to a heavy basswood cord, which was then attached to the horizontal cross-piece. The weaver would stand in front of the loom and pass the horizontal strips—the woof—over and under the first strips which would be hanging down vertically.

On occasion the Ojibwa also wove bags and baskets, but birchbark was so prevalent that this type of weaving was not done to any great extent. Birchbark supplied the material for a great many utensils, containers, and holders, and from it the Indians also made a type of rattle for ceremonial purposes, which they filled with tiny pebbles to produce the required sound effects.

The Ojibwa made two types of drum. The first, a hand-held one, was simply made and consisted of a piece of rawhide stretched over a wooden hoop and laced tightly on the reverse side. The second type was made from a section of log and was much larger. The

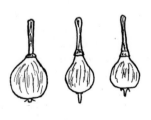

log would be partially hollowed out by charring and gouging. A hole would be bored through one side connecting with the hollow interior, and a plug inserted. The drum itself would be made fully secure by taping around the outside. The drumhead would be made of deerskin and would be held in place over the open end of the drum by means of a hoop. Before use, the drum would be filled with water and left to soak until thoroughly tightened. Then the plug would be removed and the water drained out. The plug would then be reinserted. If after the soaking the head still did not fit on tightly enough for the drum to produce the desired degree of reverberation, the drum would be held near an open fire and warmed until the right sound effect was produced. The only other musical instrument the Ojibwa made was the flagelot, or simple flute, and this was carved from cedar, ash, box elder, or sumac. It was made with six finger-holes.

Wood was also used to make such utensils as spoons, bowls, ladles, clubs, and yokes. Bone was used to make

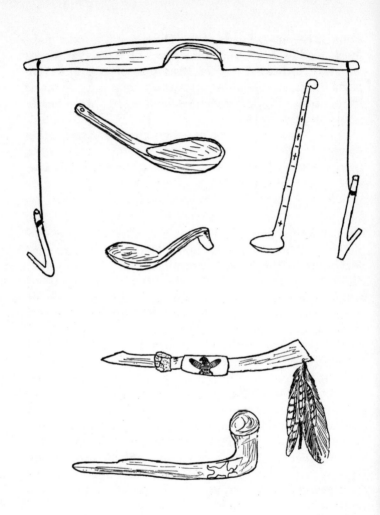

some of the arrowheads of the Ojibwa and also to make awls, needles, hoes, and some types of knives. Stone, as we have indicated earlier, was one of the most important, if not the most important, material. From it the Ojibwa chipped their axes and adzes, arrowheads, scrapers, and knives.

Stone was also used for making pipes. As among other tribes, the Ojibwa would hollow out their pipe bowls by the processes of pecking, grinding, and drilling. One type of pipe was made from the redstone of the region which was similar to the Catlinite redstone used by the Indians of the prairies. These pipes were large, and were smoked by the men. They were the so-called "peace pipes," and were smoked on ceremonial occasions as a symbol of mutual obligation between individuals. It is important to note that it was the tobacco and not the pipes which was significant on such occasions. The tobacco, as the gift of the spirits, contained magical powers. It enabled the Ojibwa to evoke the spirits, and to make thank offerings to them. These ceremonial pipes had long stems—sometimes three feet in length—which would be elaborately decorated and decked out with eagle feathers.

For everyday smoking, pipe bowls would be hollowed from a type of black stone similar in texture to the redstone, or hollowed from knotty pieces of wood, or even from sections of antler. The stems were short and detachable and made from pithy woods such as hazel. When white trade goods appeared the Indian would decorate their stone pipes by cutting slots in them to form geometric patterns, and they would fill these slots with lead.

In the matter of clothing, the Ojibwa were simple dressers, the materials they used consisting chiefly of animal hides. A woman's dress was simple in the extreme and was made by sewing two deerskins together. A hole would be left for the neck to pass through, and seams were stitched across to enclose the shoulders. The dress would be tied at the waist with a rawhide belt. To complete their costume the women would wear knee-length leggings and moccasins, also made of deerskin.

A man's garb was also simple: he would wear a short breech cloth, thigh-length leggings, and moccasins. In winter both men and women protected themselves from the cold with coats which they made from strips of rabbit's fur.

Thread, as we have seen, could be made from nettle fibre, but it was also made from the sinews which are to be found along the backbones of moose and deer. Sewing was done with sharp thorns or bone awls by the women, who also cut out the animal hides and prepared them for sewing. Every woman kept her sewing equipment and threads in a special bag which she made for this purpose.

Ojibwa moccasins were characterized by puckered seams, and some authorities maintain that the word "Ojibwa" itself is a corruption of the tribal word for "puckered." Other experts, however, feel that the word is derived from the tribal word for "painting." In winter the Indians would line their deerskin moccasins with strips of tanned muskrat hide on which the hair had been retained for additional warmth. They would decorate their moccasins with floral patterns which they would sew on with moose hair and, after the coming of the white traders, with brightly coloured beads.

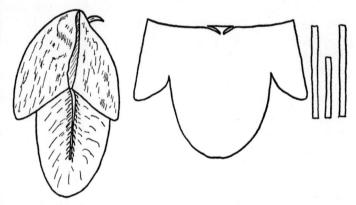

Both men and women were fond of necklaces, which they made from fresh-water clam shells or from berries which had been dried and polished, or even from the toe bones of animals, claws, the leg and wing bones of birds, or the hind legs of rabbits. Older men were fond of earrings, which, after the white man came, they made from bunches of small metal cones, which they suspended from holes pierced in the lobes of their ears.

In contrast to their simple dress, the Ojibwa made great use of ornamental sashes, leggings, and head ornaments, especially on ceremonial occasions. They would also paint their faces in a variety of coloured patterns, first painting the designs on the palms of their hands with coloured soils which they had ground to powder and mixed with grease. They would then apply their hands to their faces and thus transfer the patterns.

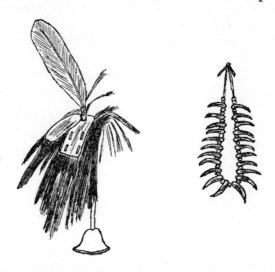

To an Ojibwa a fine head of hair was a source of great pride, and to achieve this he would spend a great deal of time over his grooming. Quite often he would call in his womenfolk to help him. To keep his hair smooth and sleek he would apply bear grease and deer tallow. When combed his hair would hang down in braids on both sides of his face, but would be cut at

CHATTERTON FALLS

On a trip in the summer of 1954. *From left to right*: Dr. Omond
Solandt, (then) Chairman, Defence Research Board, Ottawa, (now)
Assistant Vice-President for Development and Research, Canadian
National Railways, Montreal; A. H. J. Lovink, Netherlands Ambassador
to Canada; Blair Fraser, Ottawa Editor of *Maclean's Magazine*; John
Endemann, Deputy High Commissioner for South Africa

THE END OF A PORTAGE

On the Maligne River. *From left to right*: Dr. Omond Solandt; Eric Morse, National Director of the Association of Canadian Clubs; John Endemann; Blair Fraser

the front to leave a fringe across his forehead. He would keep the braids in place with beaded bands. Older men preferred elaborate hair styles, sometimes with small braids at the temples and larger ones at the sides. They would allow these to hang down, or might prefer to tie them up on the top of their heads. Decorative effects were also gained by placing feathers in the hair and by wearing, on ceremonial occasions, moosehair brooches. Ultrafashionable dandies would even add strips of yellow or red materials to their braids.

The Ojibwa were an artistically inclined people, as those readers will realize who have seen the variety of handicraft work made by modern Ojibwa in many parts of northern Ontario—handicrafts which are survivals of their own artistic heritage. In days gone by they would decorate almost everything they made or owned in some fashion. Generally they employed two basic patterns, one based on straight lines and the other on floral designs, the former representing the earlier motif. They used moosehair and porcupine quills for this decorative work, and made their colours from vegetable dyes. They turned readily to the white traders' many-coloured beads, which were much easier to use for embroidery, and, during the past three centuries, their beadwork has become internationally famous, particularly their belts and sashes, which they made on simple, hand-held looms.

Birchbark transparencies were also a favourite, and the possible artistic combinations were almost limitless. The artist would begin with a square cut from a thin layer of birchbark. He would fold it according to the pattern which he wished to create. He would then bite

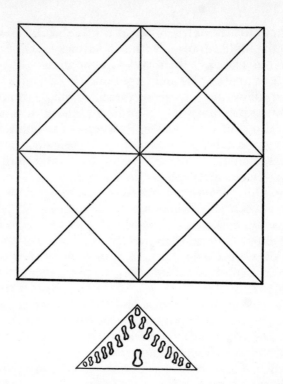

along the folds so that, when unfolded again, the square would reveal the finished pattern in full symmetry.

The most intriguing form of ancient Ojibwa art to us is the pictograph or rock painting—a number of which can be seen by modern canoe travellers in Quetico Park. They are usually to be found in such sheltered places as on the undersides of rocks which hang out over the water. These rock paintings are always small, and the individual pictures or graphs are seldom more than twelve inches in length or breadth. They have probably been painted on the rocks with a mixture of hematite (a ferrous iron oxide) and fish oil. The colour is always red.

The rock paintings depict the natural objects which the Indians observed around them, objects which include birds, animals, the sun, the moon, and human beings. They are drawn either in conventional or in stylized form. It is assumed, because of their locations, that the artists were in the habit of standing up in their canoes to execute their work.

What do these pictographs represent? No one knows for certain, but it is likely that they were associated with magical or religious symbolism. Since they are to be found so far from the beaten tracks, it is possible that they represent or record the dreams which the Ojibwa had when fasting to establish contact with their supernatural guardian spirits, an aspect of their religious life which we shall describe later.

One of the most interesting examples of rock paintings is to be found about one mile north of Lower Basswood Falls on Crooked Lake. The site is often called "Picture Rock." The rock is on the west side, where the lake is narrow and tortuous, with high rocky banks, and the paintings may be seen where the faces of these cliffs overhang the water. They include representations of men, canoes, suns, moons, moose, loons, and pelicans. Though pelicans, of course, are no longer to be found in the region.

The Ojibwa Indians, as we have pointed out, did not control their environment, but we are now able to see that they *knew* their environment. They had a precise knowledge of woods and they had mastered techniques which enabled them to make tools and implements from stone. They made their clothing from the skins of the animals of the forest. In brief, they made the most of the materials at their disposal, a fact which has a very close bearing on their attitude toward their natural surroundings.

The World of the Supernatural

WE HAVE, up to this point, seen something of the practical side of Ojibwa life. It was a difficult life at best, and the threat of starvation haunted Ojibwa families from birth to death. But in spite of this their life had its attractive side and it had its rewards. We may find this difficult to comprehend, accustomed as we are to the comforts and luxuries which our commercial and industrial civilization has provided for us. But our needs and desires, our objective and outlook are not those of all peoples of the world. We must remember that comforts and luxuries were not things which the Ojibwa desired, and that they regarded excess possessions as nuisances. We must also remember that the Ojibwa, though they did not control their environment, were well adjusted to it—and accepted it. If, in some manner, they had been transplanted to alien surroundings, they would have been most uncomfortable, just as we would be if we were to be thrust suddenly into their life. In this survey of life in the Quetico we have encountered the supernatural at almost every turn. This aspect of Ojibwa life was vital indeed, and constituted an important part of their adjustment to their environment. The mere ability to survive—which in itself was no mean achievement in seventeenth-century Quetico—

was not enough, it could not ensure the future; and it was precisely this insurance that the Ojibwa, dependent as they were upon the flora and fauna of the region, needed most. In their precarious existence in this wilderness these Indians simply had to know that the maple sap would run next spring, that the fish would not swim away, that the deer, moose, and bear would stay in the forest, and that the wild rice would be heavy on the stalks when the wild rice moon rose again in the autumn sky. These things were beyond the control of man, and lay in the domain of the spirits. Only the spirits could keep the world of the Ojibwa of the Quetico in balance, and consequently only the spirits could bring any degree of certainty to the future. It was this realm of the supernatural which gave meaning to Ojibwa life—and which made life in the Quetico possible for these Indians.

The Ojibwa believed that their world was governed by a number of spirits, including a somewhat vague and distant Supreme Being or Great or Kind Spirit whom they called Gitche Manitou (the spelling may vary). Powerful as this Great Spirit was, the Ojibwa believed that he seldom intervened directly in the affairs of their own daily lives. Rather, he delegated his powers to lesser spirits who would act as his intermediaries. There were many of these lesser spirits and they were to be found everywhere—in the living creatures of the forest, the waters, the sky, and in the inanimate objects which formed the background or setting for animal and human life. Thus the world of the Indians was both a natural and a supernatural one. The two aspects had to work together in mutual harmony lest, in the eyes of the Ojibwa, both should collapse.

How did the Ojibwa establish contact with this world of the supernatural which was so important to them? There were a number of ways, and one of the most important was through the medium of dreams. The importance of dreams was impressed upon children as they approached maturity, and it could well be said that at this stage in an Ojibwa's life dreaming was almost as purposeful an activity as any of the normal round.

It will be remembered that parents were anxious to have an Indian who had proved himself the possessor of great spirit power bestow his name upon their child as a special ceremonial name. Bestowing such a name would give the child the capacity to possess a powerful spirit himself, though the child's particular spirit would not reveal itself until he was reaching maturity. The spirit would appear to the youth in a dream, in the guise of some bird or animal, and such a manifestation or revelation would be an intense and personal experience which the young Ojibwa would remember vividly for the rest of his life.

Dreams were encouraged by fasting, which was regarded as a means of approaching the supernatural. In fact the Ojibwa believed it was only as a result of extreme privation that the spirits would reveal themselves to humans, for they would take pity on Indians who had fasted almost to the point of death.

When dreams were experienced as a result of fasting, the youths—boys or girls—would tell their parents, for it was the parents who decided which were the important and significant dreams. Any which had anything to do with birds or animals or which were considered in any way unusual were carefully noted.

Then, if a pattern seemed to be appearing in the dreams —if, for example, an eagle were to swoop down and instruct the dreamer in methods of hunting or curing disease—then it would be a sure sign that the dreamer's guardian spirit was revealing itself—in this instance in the form of an eagle. When this happened the youth would try and find—in this case—an eagle, and remove from it some part such as its tail feathers. He would place these in a special leather pouch which he would hide in a secret place.

When the young Indian needed spirit power to accomplish a specific task he would attach his pouch to his clothing and go forth on whatever venture he was about to undertake, fully confident that his guardian spirit would work with him to ensure success.

The Ojibwa believed that animals had their own particular spirit power. The majestic flight of the eagle, for example, demonstrated this bird's specific abilities. Some animals were considered, from this point of view, to possess more power than others, and when they appeared in dreams were rated accordingly. These beliefs concerning animals undoubtedly accounted generally for the importance of animals as symbols in the dreams of the Ojibwa. Some dream patterns were considered good omens for future success, and on the strength of such dreams the Ojibwa would predict their future. There would be those who would be destined to become great hunters, or inventors of new remedies, or craftsmen. However, other Indians would not find any basis for believing that they would have any special destinies: they would simply become useful members of society.

The focal point of Ojibwa religious beliefs lay in the

activities of the Midewiwin, or the Grand Medicine Society. To these Indians unusual happenings in life, including sickness, were thought to be the work of evil spirits. Sickness was also regarded as a kind of penalty for untoward acts. Therefore medical practices became intimately associated with the supernatural. Health was a fundamental concern to the Ojibwa. Their division of labour was completely individualistic and exclusive: the men engaged only in hunting and trapping and the women pursued only the many household duties. The result was that the good health of both men and women was absolutely essential to the success of the family, especially during the long periods of isolation. It was necessary, therefore, that the members of every family know something about medicine and the curing of disease. Membership in the Grand Medicine Society ensured the possession of such knowledge.

The Grand Medicine Society can be regarded as Ontario's first medical society. Although it was formed long before the first white man came, its aim was the same as that of medicine and medical societies today— the safeguarding and prolonging of human life. The Ojibwa believed this aim could be achieved in two ways: through a thorough knowledge of herbs and their medical uses and through good conduct. The men and women of the Midewiwin were called upon to observe a strict ethical code: lying and stealing were considered serious offences and erratic behaviour of any kind was most definitely to be avoided. Members were obliged to behave with decorum at all times, and hasty actions, the showing of anger, or engaging in violence were especially frowned upon.

Medicine ceremonies were held in the late spring and

early fall when the Ojibwa families could be found living together in small communal encampments. There were two ways of becoming a member of the Society. The first was as a result of illness which had necessitated calling in members of the Society to effect a cure. The second method was through a dream experience in which an Indian had been advised by his guardian spirit to seek membership for his own good. Whichever way, the applicant would signify his intention by holding a feast to which he would invite his close friends and a Mide priest. During the meal the priest would consider the events leading up to the application and decide whether the signs had been favourable. If they were, the applicant would be told to procure special offerings, which he would be expected to give as presents during his initiation ceremony. When the next Mide rites were held the applicant would be inducted, and his special offerings would represent the fees payable to the Society. His fees would bring him membership and the right to learn medical lore.

The Grand Medicine Society maintained at least four degrees of membership. Each degree which was conferred upon a member would entitle him to a certain stock of medical knowledge. Higher degrees, which gave higher knowledge, called for additional fees. As a rule, the symbol of the first degree was the skin of a weasel, that of the second the skin of an owl, the third a fox, and the fourth a bear. These skins or pieces of skin would be made into pouches in which the members would keep the various medicines associated with their degrees. It is worth noting that the Ojibwa through the activities of their medicine society possessed an astounding knowledge of herbs and their medicinal values. They were familiar enough with the growth patterns of plants that they would know to gather them when the medicinal ingredients would be at their greatest potency. It has been estimated that the Ojibwa knew and used nearly four hundred separate species of plants.

The Midewiwin ceremonies were held in elongated wigwams built especially for the purpose. Some of these wigwams were said to measure over one hundred feet in length, though few would be much wider than the regular household wigwam. The ceremony usually lasted four days, and began with physical purification in a sweat lodge. Sweat baths were popular among the Ojibwa and were often also used for curing purposes. The "bath house" would be made of a number of saplings lashed together as a framework and covered over with a skin blanket, in wigwam form. Heated stones would be carried inside on forked sticks and the bather would sprinkle them with cold water and medicinal herbs. He would remain inside inhaling the vapours until he could no longer stand the steam. He would then run outside and plunge into the nearest lake or stream, immersing himself completely in the cold water.

The Midewiwin, which reached its highest development among Ojibwa south of the Great Lakes, was a secret society with deep religious significance. The initiation ceremony was a dramatization of the myth which sought to explain how the Society had been organized countless centuries ago by the spirit "Mide Manitou" who, the Ojibwa believed, had taught the ancestors of the tribe their herbal lore. In deference to this spirit Mide members would always place bits of raw tobacco in the earth whenever they removed plants for healing purposes.

The chief features of the initiation rite was the mock slaying of the candidate by the priests, after which they would restore him to life by means of their medical powers. This drama served to symbolize the belief that all Mide members so initiated would enjoy long life and find immortality in the Hereafter. During the enactment of the drama the various treatments which were associated with the candidate's degree were demonstrated and thus taught to him.

Thus we can see, in the rites of the Midewiwin, that blending of the natural and the supernatural which so characterized Ojibwa life: on the one hand the purely practical knowledge of cures to restore and preserve health, and on the other hand the intensified role of the supernatural which took the practice of medicine well beyond its practical aims by guaranteeing immortality as well.

There were other "doctors" among the Ojibwa who were believed to possess powers far beyond those of the average Indian, but such men acted individually and not as members of an organized medicine society. These shamans, as they were often called, employed many slcight-of-hand tricks to treat the sick, but they were not charlatans who deliberately set out to deceive their patients. They too needed some method of getting at the evil spirits whom the Ojibwa believed were responsible for sickness and disease, and their method was the practice of magic. Thus, such a medicine man might diagnose an illness as being the result of an evil spirit entering the patient's body. He might, in the course of his treatment, draw a wad of feathers from the sick man's body by sleight-of-hand and declare this to be the cause of the illness. However, both the medicine man and the patient would know that the feathers were simply feathers. But to them the wad of feathers would represent the evil spirit which the power of the medicine man was strong enough to remove. In other words, the doctor could exhibit in concrete fashion the cause of the ailment and this would have a tremendous psychological effect upon the patient and relieve his fears and anxiety.

Most of these shamans, who worked as individuals rather than as members of a medicine society, possessed a keen sense of observation. They were shrewd diagnosticians and depended primarily on this faculty to seek out the nature of an ailment. When such a medicine man visited a patient he would observe the pulse rate, the pupils of the eyes, the condition of the tongue, the respiration rate, body temperature, and he would enquire as to the location of pain. On the basis of his assessment of the patient's condition he would decide whether it would be necessary to prescribe or attempt an immediate treatment or whether he should endeavour to contact his spirit power for advice. The latter course was the one usually followed by shamans —who, incidentally, could be of either sex—and they would do so by dreaming or by employing what has come to be known as the "shaking tent" ceremony.

This rite would be performed in a small barrel-shaped lodge which the shaman would erect near the edge of the encampment, and which he would occupy in his attempt to commune with the spirits. This lodge would consist of a number of saplings set vertically in the ground in the shape of a small circle. The heavier end of each sapling would be implanted firmly in the ground. Smaller branches would be interlaced between the uprights horizontally, and the entire structure bound securely with basswood fibre. A skin blanket would be thrown over the framework so that the shaman would be concealed from public view. When the lodge was prepared the shaman would enter and begin to smoke. It would be usual for a number of spectators to gather and observe the proceedings from a discreet distance.

In the lodge or tent the shaman would meditate and try to contact the spirits. Sometimes the observers outside would hear a number of voices coming from within the tent, voices which would include those of the shaman, the patient, perhaps the patient's relatives and friends, and on occasion the voices of some of the spectators nearby. When the spirits were approaching, the tent would suddenly begin to shake, swaying violently from side to side. This mysterious phenomenon would indicate that the shaman was actually communing with the spirits. In reality, in spite of the fact that the lodge poles were set firmly in the ground, it was possible for the shaman—swept away with the fervour of the ritual—to shake the tent involuntarily, for the firmness of its base would give it a great degree of flexibility: it could be shaken quite violently without any danger of toppling over. The psychological effects of this shaking tent upon the spectators would be tremendous.

When the shaman had completed his conversation with the spirits the tent would become still again and the medicine man would emerge with the necessary cure for his patient clearly in mind. The shaking tent ritual would also be used for other purposes than discovering cures for sickness: it could be employed to learn the location of lost articles, to predict the future, and to learn the details of some misfortune.

The shamans performed by far the most spectacular of the curing feats practised by Ojibwa medical men. They spent a great deal of time learning their art and, as we might expect, the decision to become a shaman in the first place would come through a dream experience. When it became apparent that a young Ojibwa of either sex had an unusually powerful guardian spirit his family would make arrangements for him to receive training. He would receive this training from some relative who also happened to be a shaman or, if his relations did not include such a practitioner, from an outsider with whom suitable arrangements could be made. After training, his position as a practising shaman would be recognized and would provide him with his livelihood. Like the priests of the Midewiwin or the Grand Medicine Society, he would receive payment for his treatments.

Epilogue

THIS brings us to the end of our description of the Ojibwa Indians who once inhabited the Quetico Park region and their way of life. Today none of these people remain in the Park. The last one died just after the turn of the present century—of a white man's disease. Some of the descendants of the Ojibwa we have been discussing may still be found near the borders of the Park, but few of the customs and practices we have described are observed by them today.

With the coming of the white man the Indian way of life began to undergo changes. Today it has virtually disappeared, and with it much of the wilderness with which it was so closely associated. Serious efforts are being made to restore the latter, but the former—the seventeenth century life of the Ojibwa—has vanished for ever. It has become a part of history.

Yet the Indian's heritage has not been entirely lost to us. There are values in the wilderness life even for twentieth-century man, values which could give a balance to our outlook. As Mr. F. B. Hubachek has pointed out in his introduction to the 1949–50 Annual Report of the Quetico–Superior Research Center:

... the complexities and artificialities of modern life may destroy our civilization unless means are found to anchor us to the

54

simplicities of existence. Every year we get farther away from the realities of man's struggle against environment. Anything which can be done to keep humanity in contact with nature is worth doing. As a people our balance, perspective, and sense of values can best be preserved by retaining personal knowledge of the elemental problems of existence. This can be assisted by personal contact with wilderness country under primitive conditions.

In conserving wilderness regions such as the Quetico, then, we can reflect on the life and the outlook of the Ojibwa, its ancient inhabitants, whose values sprang from this wilderness and call to us today from across the centuries with a message we would do well to heed.

Quetico Park

QUETICO PARK lies on the Ontario–Minnesota boundary, and its eastern border is approximately ninety miles from Port Arthur, Ontario. It may be reached by Canadian National Railway or by Ontario Highway Number 120 from Fort William and Port Arthur. Information on the Park may be obtained from the Quetico Foundation, 226 Simcoe Street, Toronto 2-B, from the Ontario Department of Lands and Forests, Queen's Park, Toronto, or from the Department's District Forester, Fort Francis, Ontario.

This book has been made possible through the active co-operation of the Quetico Foundation and the Ontario Department of Lands and Forests. Readers who may wish to secure more detailed accounts of the life of the Indians of Quetico will find the list of books below of interest:

DENSMORE, FRANCES. *Chippewa Customs.* (Bureau of American Ethnology Bulletin 86.) Washington, D.C., 1929.

HOFFMAN, W. J. "The Midewiwin or 'Grand Medicine Society' of the Ojibway," *7th Annual Report of the Bureau of American Ethnology.* Washington, D.C., 1886.

JENNESS, DIAMOND. *Indians of Canada.* (Canadian Department of Mines Bulletin 65, "Anthropological Series," No. 15.) Ottawa, 1932.

JENKS, A. E. "The Wild Rice Gatherers of the Upper Great Lakes," *19th Annual Report of the Bureau of American Ethnology*, Part II. Washington, D.C., 1898.

KINIETZ, W. V. *The Indians of the Western Great Lakes, 1615–1760.* ("University of Michigan, Museum of Anthropology, Occasional Contributions," No. 10.) Ann Arbor, 1940.

LYFORD, CARRIE A. *The Crafts of the Ojibwa.* ("Indian Handcraft Series," No. 5.) Phoenix: Office of Indian Affairs, 1943.

UNDERHILL, RUTH M. *Red Man's America.* Chicago: Univ. of Chicago Press, 1953.

Acknowledgements

GRATEFUL acknowledgements are made to Robert C. Dailey, Kenneth E. Kidd, and Sigurd F. Olson, for the photographs included in this book. The endpaper map was prepared by William A. Howard, and the line drawings were made by Robert C. Dailey. The frontispiece picture of the Ojibwa camp is reproduced by special permission of Dr. Sigmund Samuel.

The book is set in Linotype Caledonia, a font designed by W. A. Dwiggins. Typography, cover, and decorations by Antje Lingner, University of Toronto Press.